Death and Remembrance

Isabel White

To Coral

Best wishes

Isabel

x

Death and Remembrance first published in April 2010 by
Alarms & Excursions
2 Holly Lodge
7 Wisteria Road
London
SE13 5HW
(www.alarmsandexcursions.com)

ISBN 978-0-9565761-0-1

Cover design by Sarah Young (www.sarahyoung.co.uk)

Printed on recycled paper by Print Resources

Lifeless you lie in the linen press,
drawers lined with faintly scented heartache...

For Fraser

ACKNOWLEDGEMENTS:

The author gratefully acknowledges the support and encouragement of the editors of a number of journals who have previously published her work, including *Succour*, *WordsMyth*, *Trespass*, *Poetry Pearl*, *The Sun Also Rises* and BBC Local Radio. The author would also like to thank Amy White whose unswerving dedication to the task of cutting out the dross has ensured that only the best make it to the final cut. Finally, a big thank you to a number of well and lesser known poets (too numerous to mention) whose constructive comment and camaraderie has endured through the dark days when the muse deserts us.

CONTENTS

1

THE MAGNIFICENT SEVEN

One less welcome outcome of the boom in London's population in the early part of the nineteenth century was the rapid decline in standards of sanitation, the onset of plagues and the overcrowding of existing burial sites. These problems reached crisis point within a few years, resulting in the government creating, by act of parliament, the concept of privatised garden cemeteries. In 1832 parliament passed the 'Act for Establishing a General Cemetery for the Interment of the Dead in the Neighbourhood of the Metropolis', which led to the establishment of seven major burial sites, located in what was then the periphery of the city. The first of these, Kensal Green Cemetery, was swiftly followed by sites at Norwood, Highgate, Nunhead, Brompton, Abney Park and Tower Hamlets. These remain today as magnificent, though often careworn and forgotten memorials to Victorian culture and ingenuity.

They are in most cases, havens for wildlife and tranquil spaces of great beauty. They are also home to some of the most ludicrously named individuals and families that ever walked the streets of our capital. Being christened Eulalia Cattermole was just as likely to result in the death of your dynasty as any predisposition to disease or dodgy genetics...

Monument in Kensal Green Cemetery. Photo: Andrew Moffatt

KENSAL GREEN

As a gloom of Goths descends,
I hear a rumour, parasols in bloom
and the flit-flat taffeta's swish,
gliding over the tomb,
of Lucifer's patissière,
as she ices the iron and stone confections
and hangdog delights of Kensal.

With a face to die for,
this coquettish come on,
wasted at the nip,
disports her corset,
litters the lawns,
monochrome star of the Chronicle,
she is Victoria's Secret!

I believe I have the measure of her at last,
not yet undead, but nevertheless apprenticed…
and most at her leisure, whiling away her days
in illustrious company
with Hertudes, who concluded
on a wind tossed sunny Sunday,
when the trees whispered - Shh!
Just like now.

Ms Goth darts from tomb to tomb, a Transylvanian raven,
beak sharp and predatory. I almost see her.
I go every Sunday now,
hoping for a glimpse of her, resurrecting another,
Chrisostome Monflet (dead as a Saturday chip),
while the sun, through her black lace parasol,
tattoos her ashen face.

The spectre of her accomplice, the Judderman,
liquorice lipped, buckled, zipped and stayed,
lurks by the hearse.
She reclines like pumice on Stromboli,
as hoards of sinning bats
scatter in the encroaching twilight.

As the waxing moon ta dahs and grimaces,
I'm startled by the hoot of the night's first raptor.
She, "Paging Mr Death!"
He, ever the predator.

NORWOOD

Evidently, the way in for the mortal
is through this palm-fringed portal;
repose for those with more cash to splash.

Now lovers and liars
and high rollers pause
with their strollers;
the man from the council
worse than useless with who lies where,
but OK with shoots and leaves
for the bereaved.

In back by the crem'
it's all Greek to me,
Ralli, Scaramanga and Rodocanachi,
peeps within and without the private chapel grounds;
Theognosia Charalambous was not famous
despite the way she sounds.

Everyone dies here euphemistically,
some are *called away*
others *fall asleep.*
You'd think, having had a long lie-in
they'd want to be up and doing.

I shall linger
where the finger of ivy-entwined fate
has sealed Henry Doulton and Mr Tate.
I shall potter to where in matching terracotta
they got shot of their mortal coils;
I shall do them in ink
while others do them in oils.

As for the rest,
loved ones come quietly to pray

Until the day dawns
And the shadows flee away.

MENAGERIST
(Highgate West Cemetery)

Saved by the bell
(so I hear tell),
they lie, pell mell,
head to toe,
cheek to cheek,
up the hill,
down the dale;
get Dalziel to tell their tale in stone,
as he told of Alice
and those acquainted with Mr Dickens
(it obviously served him well).

Gonna rent me a real estate,
a tomb with a view on Egyptian Avenue
where models of decorum and decomposure
can dance round the cedar,
perfect for the Paiute
arranged by Rosa.

Snow drops on snowdrops
where, from the well of loneliness,
finally,
Marguerite (Love that hat!)
found fast friends to tend her,
those who will not betray by bedding, then wedding,
as was the tradition
in her day.

Nearest to God lies Julius,
his pigeons only here for the bier.
Marvel at the marble,
no one else does today,

save for curious tourists
who will forget the tall tales
of Wallis the lion,
two boa constrictors
"Can you see them on the trolley?"
a penny a look
'cos there was no picture in any book
and slippery Wombwell
paying handsome
(some say a king's ransom)
for board and lodging for his kangaroo.

On the path to the gate
Jesus Christ
(No, not him - the druid's son)
and other boxes
are stacked in the Columbarium.

Caitlin
Love you forever

Postscript
(Highgate East Cemetery)

Three Japanese men lined up beneath Karl Marx
Three Japanese men in coats from Marks and Sparks
And if one Japanese man accidently carks
There'll be two Japanese men lined up beneath Karl Marx

JOURNEY TO THE CITY OF LOOS

If Bazalgette hadn't given in to bricks!

We would come to this place on high days and holidays;
join the ponging throng
headed for the fragrant city on yonder hill,
Shitopolis.
Once through the gates and greeted by an army of flunkies
we would be guided to our own private palace of poo,
all carved marble and cast iron,
that many splendoured place
that stood cheek by jowl, or in our case, cheek by cheek
with our neighbours,
where we would pass the time of day
(and plenty else besides).
All around, men and women would bob up and down to admire their handiwork,
the ladies hidden behind filigree screens which allowed for conversation
(which is what most women do when they are on the loo)
but maintained their modesty,
and the chaps, lined up in Byzantine urinals
would stand in thrall of their neighbours' priapus in the next door stall
or be regaled by tales of jobbing plumbers
with the squits…

For the hoi polloi, rows of cubicles stretched to the horizon
and at intersections the brush boys,
apprenticed to the lavatory man (who, naturally, had the moniker of Dan)
would be sent round the u-bends
to ensure that all was spic and span.
In the central square, stood an unctuous monument to Thomas the king of crap,

given the clap he by now so richly deserved
in celebration of such glorious sanitation.

The quacks, whose formulations to ease constipation
or devices to fill crevices,
vied for the attention of those in a hurry
to settle their scores with Montezuma
(out for revenge as usual),
and in the corner, the cottage,
reserved for the friends of young Michael,
who had other agendas to pursue
so had their own private loo.

And a century on,
when so public and social an evacuation
was no longer favoured by this nation,
the weeds would take hold,
goldfish no longer swim in the copper and glass cisterns on Dump Street
and the Friends of the City of Loos
would charge me a penny, to sit in contemplation, broken-hearted
and dream of gases now departed.

ORATORY IN WEST BROMPTON

Shall we dine with kings and princes,
fetch up in a stretch Hummer
in all its tawdry glory,
set our pyre of faggots,
lure maggots to be picked over by pigeons,
cowed by crows?

Tell me, what price honour, these days?
Remembrance?
What price those?

Heh, John Nevil Maskelyne
close neighbour of Lysacht Pennefat,
how do you handle that?

Say, Mam'selle Theophile
Aime Arsene Noel,
your Christmases all come at once,
yet still you succumb
to a surfeit of overwrought nomenclature.

Eulalia,
you rest so close to Bliss
and Horace, that's your Lott in the family plot
hard by Dear Little Judy,
off to meet her wizard.

Tell me, seventeen admirals,
backs to the wall,
now you navigate your own private Styx,
your way to the sea barred by bricks
like Cunard's grave, and Inderwick's;

tell me, do you still go down to the sea in ships?
Are your names on the lips of sailors,
now pressganged by the reaper's crew,
brought low by age or some ancient ague?

Generals,
now your guns are stilled,
your salients conquered;
beneath the starless skies
we mortals, fearful your new armies will arise,
build a bridgehead
between us and the dead.

Sing to me Tauber,
on the joys of life
now you have passed over.

Emmeline, declaim as only a dame can,
on the perils of leaving voting to a man.

Now sunset trashes the mackerel sky,
scatters the ashes of the day.
In contemplation,
a wife tends her husband's path to salvation;
all the while the boys come and go,
copping off
while you and I are popping off.

LI'L ABNEY

Sunday's you'll find me
tilting at Harriet.
Judas Iscariot is not here,
least not in the flesh.
But many a soul is, ...or was,
on finding themselves bereft of a body.

Maddy's here
and Ronnie's Daddy.
Don't forget the General and Mrs. B
bigging it up by the gate
in granite and slate.

Apostles jostle for miniscule plots
of earth that man and time forgot;
foxes, squirrels and worms,
on squelching terms with slothful slugs
and headless angels, haunt the undergrowth.
Seth and Lavinia are in the pink,
or under it at least.

While the crows feast,
eyeing the boomtown rats,
the old man goes cruising in his titfer.

As an antidote to Abney
and its solemnity
you can gaze at the fancies in Rosa's corset shop
on the corner,
or salsa and merenge on rainy days
in the tangerine gaze of the tapas bar
that sold its Sol to the devil.

With her dying breath,
Emily Moxsom penned the Tropic Death;
now she is merely jetsam,
as transient as Big Dave
whose gusset is remembered in Another Place
on a more unlikely grave.

Before departing,
as a penance,
I shall put the Hasidic Jews on notice
to conjure for me, a wreath of stephanotis.

TOWER HAMLETS

To chill the blood icier than an arctic day
they come, promenading,
pallid waifs in gowns to sweep the leaf strewn labrynth,
on the arms of putty faced pall bearers, top hatted to a man.
Every one redolent of their fetid end,
a mad carnival of sweet terror,
they sweep me up with their dishevelled revels
and as swiftly as they had come,
segue through the trees
to an ominous quiet.

I follow
entranced;
for today the dead are abroad,
their grimace
startling the rooks
exploding through the leprous knuckles of gnarled oaks.

Ten thousand shadows jostle for bedspace;
hearts torn out,
souls not so much in torment
as eternal indolence,
doll eyed and lolling.

Stillness reigns,
save for the chill to my bones
and the dead white hand on my shoulder.

TIME OUT IN AN INNSBRUCK FRIEDHOF

(Great cemeteries are not just confined to London. Here is another of my favourites...)

They all reproach me silently…
We are black granite and gilt letters,
iron and marble…
Be still a while…
Take stock…

Hans Kalas, dentist
In Frieden, Richard Hüber, Trafikant

A lizard surfs the pebbles,
darts down a tomb.
Flowers and alpines
combine
between the shadows.

Hier rüht in Gott
Paula Landa, geboren Wachter

A heather clad figure
is hunched over a tomb,
white hair billowing softly.
Reverence is fresh cut flowers…

The tram beckons with its clanging bell;
there is more living to do.

II

Edwin Starr's Grave, West Bridgford, Nottinghamshire. Photo: The Author

AGENT OO SOUL

I met you once
and saw your show
at least twice more.

And when you died
I cried to think we'd let you go so soon,
(fifty gigs, and that, in one year alone).

You were the brother they named soul after
but after Edwin, there could be no other.
Your suppositions about war
(we all know about that)
but death?
Good God, what is that good for?
Absolutely nothing.

Still, it's headline news
about how happy you have made me.
You know my weakness has always been you.
You'll still be missed most everywhere;
in Polesworth,
and wherever the groove is rare.
Anywhere you can hear the happy radio
make contact, you've twenty-five miles still to go.
(It's much, much further from Maine to Mexico)

ROMANCING THE SLOANE

Thirty years before..., the Flask...
You, yes you with your quiet pint,
you never knew
Spigot's tormentor;
gaunt and haunted,
Wisty whenever she was near,
colluding with his latest tow haired temptress
hung on his every bon mot.

Lothario
through the window,
I spied him,
schmoozing,
gatecrashed his manoeuvres,
back when flat caps, slack jaws and whippets ruled the day,
no goons with foie gras and prunes
to eat in or take away.

Now beyond the fringes of Theatreland
frail alumnus Alan soldiers on alone
while he's up in heaven
romancing another Sloane.

ALAS POOR DIBNAH, I KNEW HIM HORATIO

Fresh from her heavy bottom end repair
we lit her up at dawn, yesterday,
prepped for t' last grand tour,
cross heads remachined,
gudgeon pins, *gudged*, cotter pins *er, cotted*,
side stays replaced and then she were fit.

Shrouded in black lace,
nipples greased up,
rubber belts whirrin' and whoopin', blowin' off,
spoke plates and balance weights
burnished to buggery,
injector primed and ready…

this waking November, we're off.
A beacon of hope in this dark satanic world,
the fireman's brazier burning bright
an eternal flame for Fred
who despite protestations to t' contrary
is alas, very dead.

And so, at last, will it actually run then?
The lone engineer pipes an oily lament
to the Bolton Baudelaire of nuts and bolts,
Sultan of the spanner, spire and steeple,
mechanistic meccano man of the people,
he reigns in steam supreme.

BASQUE COUNTRY

Scarlet and black, it hangs behind the door,
lace and bones and suspenders.
Doris, who is eighty-four,
tries it on,
remembers.

JAZZ WALLAH

Well all right then!
One take wonder in Tin Pan Alley,
Fats scats with coolest cats,
tongue tripped spliffed riffs,
bones nipped and tucked,
as other jazzers lucked out.

In clear and present pleasure
by turns Fats yearns and gurns,
late syncopator
My very good friend
We fell in love with you.

In swashbuckling swing, mid-take,
sweet wine of Adaline
just getting into your Stride,
its all over,
All that meat and no potater
See *ya later, alligator.*

LET'S GO AWAY FOR A WHILE

Van Dyke normally shoots from the lip.
He parked his muse for this one;
Brian's pet sound, base harmonica,
an echo wrapped in skyscrapers,
downtown lights drawn in cotton candy
on velvet nights,
a solo in a concrete landscape.

He whistles in some Theremin for Dennis,
for Carl.
I hear his knock
ricocheting off the streets.
No one's up,
not even the surf.
Forever 3 a.m.

Where the kids aren't hip any more,
he is home in bed,
some dope's helmet upturned,
brimful of quavers,
minims and several bars rest.

In the Congress Theatre
thirty years away,
a windowless room,
expressionless face,
nice thought.

III

Fraser in Buffalo N Y, 1942. Photo: Unknown

CHATEAU FRASER

Not long after he died
I would find him behind the bread bin,
keeping an eye.

In those days he was pristine,
gold paper seal,
hand painted label.

The art of home brew,
a kit bought from Boots,
not the last one he made.

He must have been in the cellar
beneath the cobwebs
when we wet the babies' heads.

At the christening,
in the rush,
we let him down by forgetting.

I was doing the life laundry,
found an old friend,
the ink fading fast.

Years later I dusted him down.
Made another promise I didn't keep.
Put him back on the shelf.

Moving house, again
and again,
packed and unpacked…

Maybe for my fortieth...
At our twenty fifth...
Celebrating the divorce...

My civil servant in the cupboard,
limited edition
(the label is missing).

On duty, still,
(How many cupboards he's seen!)
I've left him to the kids in my will.

IN MEMORIAM, PATCH & ALLINGHAM

You rightly hang your head in shame,
Soldiers of Stone.

You stand guard
over the fallen,
those undeterred, through valour
now interred through callous disregard.

You cannot hold a candle to them,
Patch and Allingham.

Why did they live so long?
Maybe to atone for lives cut short,
exhausted in the trying, they too are gone.

IN FADING LIGHT

Was it windsong,
a trick of the light,
the whisper of Merlin feathering?

Hardest of all to wait behind,
again and again to say your goodbyes
to all those soldiers of the skies
drowning in blood,
oil in their throats,
tears in your eyes.

FIELD STATION

On the gentle hills of Picardy
we wait at the field station,
jackets off, braces hung,
legs outstretched,
boots unlaced,
as the sun lifts over the trees.

Our arms aloft,
ears of corn
waving at the skylark,
we are a thousand shining roses
captured in song;
we are soldiers thinking of England.

A century on,
I'm striding across the downs,
see a thousand poppies
in a field of corn,
reflecting…
I am England thinking of soldiers.

ON THE MENIN GATE

Princess Patricia's C L I
came to Wipers,
came to die.
Pals at their side,
they fought and died,
gained a few yards,
they fought and died.
Hussar and Sepoy,
Carabinier,
Severed Leg and Fusilier,
fifty-five thousand
listed here.

LIMITED EDITIONS

Sun behind you
so it frames your subject -
hot metal, kerosene,
flesh and bone and iron will.
This is the school
that drew the artists...
each perfecting their art, their skill
in the skies over Biggin Hill.

Hold still,
while I trace in pencil and gouache,
your face, half blown away.
How artless must it be
to live to fight another day.

IV

Georges Krins, 1st violin on the R.M.S. Titanic, Spa, Belgium. Photo: The Author

MR ISMAY'S BOAT

Corralled in steerage, they celebrate, Davey Jones fashion
with whatever implement comes to hand,
the promise of a new life
in a new land
fulfilled,
in a place where sea worms hold sway
and comestibles lie strewn over the sand.

So many cabin doors shut tight this morning.
No murmur of maids.
No scurry of flunkeys.
No one stirs, not even Isidor
or his adoring Frau Straus,
still tucked up
in her furs.

The captain's table beckons.
Indeed Mr Smith already holds court
(Mrs Smith waits at home, for news).
All will be welcome now
above or below decks,
passengers and crew alike.
(I heard seven hundred jumped ship last night)

There is much talk of the party.
So much carousing in the sea
in flowing frocks, jewels bobbing on the waterline.
I swore I saw my gown float by
on a mermaids arm.
And was that you I spied in a tipsy boat,
before the rest of the revellers tipped up, shipped out?

Of course not.
Here you are taking the air with me,
what's left of it;
this great ship, bilious and recalcitrant
too early to bed, amid tears and tantrums.
Now, where shall we be on the 16th,
nearer my God to thee or two miles deep?

We slipped earth's anchor yesterday.
Mr Chapman tells me the watch stopped
when she took her dive.
He says it will always be
one forty-five.

Fathoms deep the dowager lies
and many besides.

THE GLASS AND CARD METHOD

Junior ranks are excused.
I fear the repercussions
of a higher authority.

As for the rest,
once you can see their muscles...
Well, we have this agreement.
They stay out of my way,
I stay out of theirs.
It's a territorial thing.

Every so often
someone breaks the rules
(its rarely me).

I used to show no mercy,
whacked the little bastards' brains out
with a slipper.

Age has however taught me
perhaps there is no malice
in their transgression.

The receptacle has to be glass,
so I can see them in it.

They must be dropped from a great height
(I know it can't hurt them).

FREE CLIMBER

She climbed free;
free from the ties that bind us to the earth,
skating over overhangs,
death hanging over her.
No one defies gravity quite like the French.
They have an affinity for death-defying deftness,
a sleight of hand over land,
and death it seems
indulges them,

but only momentarily

BLANK CANVAS

On the face of it
we paint our own picture,
only mine has an old master
under it.

Rarely commissioned, we paint for ourselves,
wife, mother, nurse, helpmate, confidante...

We camouflage each other until we forget
how the blank canvas looked
when we were apprenticed,

and nobody's buying.

WATCHING THE SKYE
(For Elvis)

If only Charlie had a trailer at Culloden,
an Airstream
all steel and chrome
that no musket ball could pierce or broadsword fierce
rend asunder.
He would be safe inside,
at home with the essentials
for baking, making cullen skink,
the stink of skirlie and stovies all around him,
his sullen brigades waging unwinnable war,
Cumberland enraged
and despite him a crack shot with clapshot,
destiny against him.

Yon Charlie, (lately jilted by our Flora,
her sonsie face turned longingly to his,
in awe of his barely concealed culinary credentials)
the while, sings this lonely lament...

Ah Yes, I'm the Young Pretender
Pretending that I am in charge
My need is such
Of cake, I've too much
I'm out there, giving it large
With flour, egg yolks and marge...

To this day,
on windswept sites all over the coast
caravans are parked in reverence,
as if searching for Charlie's ghost.

To a man, Scots from every clan,
gather from hither and thither;
should the tilt of their kilts be out of kilter,
ensure that they hang level and do not bevel,
and in the ensuing Dash of White Sergeants
Virginia Reels and Flora's Fancy,
remember the ghost of Charlie's appearances
on mony occasions during the clearances.

THE GARAGE POET (LAUGHARNE)

The ink barely dry on the Riot Act,
Caitlin lays it aside and prepares the roast.
Dylan meanwhile, holds them in thrall
in the bloody assizes of Brown's Hotel,
raises a toast while raising hell
and lays the ghost of the Bladdered Bard of Buggerall.

Do not go gentle into that good fight,
stay where the words and the whisky blend,
be oblivious to oblivion,
make free with the spirits of Manhattan and Ceredigion,
only go back when its sloe black, crow black night.

Up the hill at St Martin's,
her moniker forever faces America.
His is turned toward the good Welsh earth,
land of his fathers, land of his birth.
Just like Watkins and Augustus John
Quite Early One Morning... he was gone.

NOTES TO THE POEMS IN THIS VOLUME

Readers may be interested to know some of the references used in the poems in this volume (others I am keeping to myself)...

Kensal Green – Kensal Green, along with all the Magnificent Seven cemeteries, is a popular resort for the Goth community who carry on the Victorian tradition of promenading in these beautiful places. You may often see them arrive in large motor hearses, the American models being particularly spectacular. The *News Chronicle* was founded in 1872, being absorbed by the *Daily Mail* in 1960. H. G. Wells, G. K. Chesterton and Sir Arthur Conan Doyle were all regular contributors. Victoria's Secret is an American retailer of corsetry. The Judderman was a character in an advertisement for alcoholic products in the 1990's.

Norwood – The Greek cemetery has the most elaborate tombs in Norwood and is situated at the opposite end of the cemetery from the main gate. The final couplet of the poem can be found on the tomb of Mr Henry Tate, the sugar magnate. His tomb and that of the Royal Doulton Pottery Company's founder, Henry Doulton are both finished in terracotta.

Menagerist – By any measure, the greatest of the Magnificent Seven, a trip to Highgate is a must for all lovers of Victoriana. This poem only scratches the surface of the delights that await the visitor. Dalziel was a Victorian engraver who illustrated many of the great literary works of the age, including those by Dickens and Lewis Carroll. The Paiute were a tribe of North American Indians reputed for their communal dances in the round. The impresario Carl Rosa is buried in the Circle of Lebanon, the central ring at Highgate Cemetery, as is Marguerite Radclyffe Hall who penned *The Well of Loneliness*. Julius Beer has arguably the grandest mausoleum in the Cemetery. Highgate is also brimful of curiosities, including the grave of the menagerist (a collector and exhibitor of exotic fauna) George Wombwell, whose infamous travelling show was reputedly the inspiration for the famous monologue *Albert and the Lion* by Marriott Edgar. Postscript – This story is substantially true, but there were actually five of them, one holding the Nikon.

Journey to the City of Loos – This was the first of the Magnificent Seven poems that I was inspired to write. Given the Victorians' love of invention, pomp, and ritual, I thought it might be a nice idea to transpose the elaborate processes connected with dying with their equally elaborate processes for disposing of daily human waste. This is the (rather dubious) result, for which I can only apologise!

Oratory In West Brompton – Richard Tauber, famous for his top hat and monocle, was an Austrian tenor of international renown who appeared with many of the famous stars of the twenties and thirties, including Marlene Dietrich. He finally married an Englishwoman, Diana Napier and settled in the UK. He is buried close to Emmeline Pankhurst, leader of the British suffragette movement, near the cemetery gates.

Li'l Abney – Founders of the Salvation Army, General and Mrs. Booth are buried near the gate of Abney Park Cemetery. Big Dave's Gusset (graffiti) deserves a mention for the smile it brings to passengers on the Southeastern Railway as they journey between Waterloo East and London Bridge stations. Visit it soon, it may not be there forever. Stephanotis is a fragrant evergreen also known as Bridal Veil. Almost unknown in the UK, *Li'l Abner* was a hugely successful American comic strip, drawn by Al Capp, which ran for 43 years from 1934 to 1977. It has nothing whatsoever to do with Abney Park, which is why I corrupted it to form the title of the poem.

Tower Hamlets – This is the most careworn of the Magnificent Seven. The cemetery is no longer consecrated ground and still suffers at the hands of people who accord it little or no respect. Unlike the others, there are few celebrities of note buried here. I found it a most unsettling place.

Agent OO Soul - A number of Edwin's songs are referenced here. In case you cannot spot them, they are: *Soul*

Master, War, Headline News, Oh How Happy, My Weakness Is You, Happy Radio, Contact, 25 Miles and *Stop Her On Sight.*

Romancing The Sloane – Comedian Peter Cook frequented the Flask Inn, Highgate and I encountered him there in 1971. Mr Spigot was a character from one of the best sketches to come from his collaboration with Dudley Moore, and is also famous as both comics found it hard not to corpse during the act. E L Wisty was possibly his best known comic creation; Misty a favourite composition by Erroll Garner, especially when sung by Johnny Mathis. Along with Jonathan Miller, the fourth member of the comedy review team that created *Beyond The Fringe* was Alan Bennett. The Flask now serves foie gras with prunes, which is absolutely delicious! By the time you read this I am certain they will have changed the menu (but you never know).

Jazz Wallah – Thomas Wright 'Fat's' Waller was a master of stride piano. Again a number of his songs are referenced here.

Let's Go Away For A While – One of only two instrumentals on the *Pet Sounds* Album, this was allegedly "the most satisfying piece of music I (Brian Wilson) have ever made". Another quote from Brian refers to the poem's last line "nice thought, most of us don't go away, but it's still a nice thought". For me, *Let's Go Away For a While* is the quintessential evocation of a cool early morning (just before dawn) following a hot night in the city (to gain its full effect, listen first to the Lovin' Spoonful's version of *Summer in the City*). I met Brian in a windowless room in the Congress Theatre, Eastbourne in July 2005. He reminded me of the Manchurian Candidate.

Chateau Fraser – The photograph shows Fraser enjoying a bit of R & R during his RAF training at Navigation School in Canada.

In Memoriam, Patch & Allingham – Dedicated to Harry Patch and Henry Allingham, the last survivors of the Great War 1914-1918, who died in 2009.

Limited Editions – Dedicated to a young RAF Flight

Sergeant, an artist who drew cameos of all his fellow serving officers and men at Biggin Hill aerodrome. He was burned to death over the English Channel in 1943.

Mr Ismay's Boat – J Bruce Ismay was Chair of the White Star Line, owners of the RMS Titanic, which went down in the North Atlantic in April 1912. Isidor Straus and his wife also perished, as did Mr Chapman, although his watch survived and is frozen at the time it hit the water – 1.45 a.m. The last stanza references Ariel in Shakespeare's The Tempest *"Full fathom five thy father lies"* and the last line is an oblique reference to Charles Baudelaire's poem *Le Cygne (The Swan)*, which finishes:

I think of sailors on some isle forgotten;
Of captives, vanquished... and many more

The photograph commemorates Georges Krins (1889-1912), first violin in the Titanic band, who perished in the disaster. The Hotel Cardinal now stands on the site of his family home in the Belgian resort of Spa.

Watching The Skye – Known as Bonnie Prince Charlie or the Young Pretender, Charles Edward Stuart's army was famously defeated at the hands of the Duke of Cumberland, an event which prompted the Highland Clearances; poor families were driven off their land, which was later given or sold off to wealthy Sassenach interlopers. The poem is dedicated to the inspirational Elvis McGonagall, who is in my opinion, Britain's best satirical performance poet.

The Garage Poet (Laugharne) – A number of Dylan Thomas's poems are referenced here – you can work out which they are for yourselves – that is your homework for today, and no, the answers will not be in my next collection, coming to a cinema near you, from Sunday.